What We Leave Behind

cut-up poems and collages

Peter Wortsman

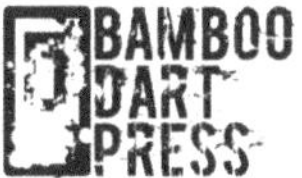

LOS ANGELES † NEW YORK † LONDON † MELBOURNE

What We Leave Behind by Peter Wortsman

978-1-962316-21-7   Paperback

978-1-962316-22-4   Ebook

Cover art, "Torn Collage, 168th Street Station, NYC, 2021," found and photographed by Peter Wortsman, image resized by Harold Wortsman

Cover design by Harold Wortsman

Layout and design by Mark Givens and Peter Wortsman

Author photograph by Jean-Luc Fievet

For information:

Bamboo Dart Press

chapbooks@bamboodartpress.com

Bamboo Dart Press 059

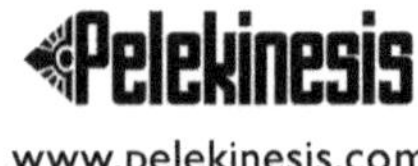

www.pelekinesis.com

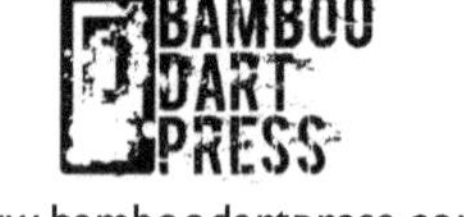

www.bamboodartpress.com

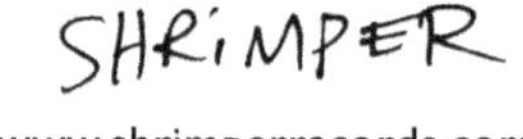

www.shrimperrecords.com

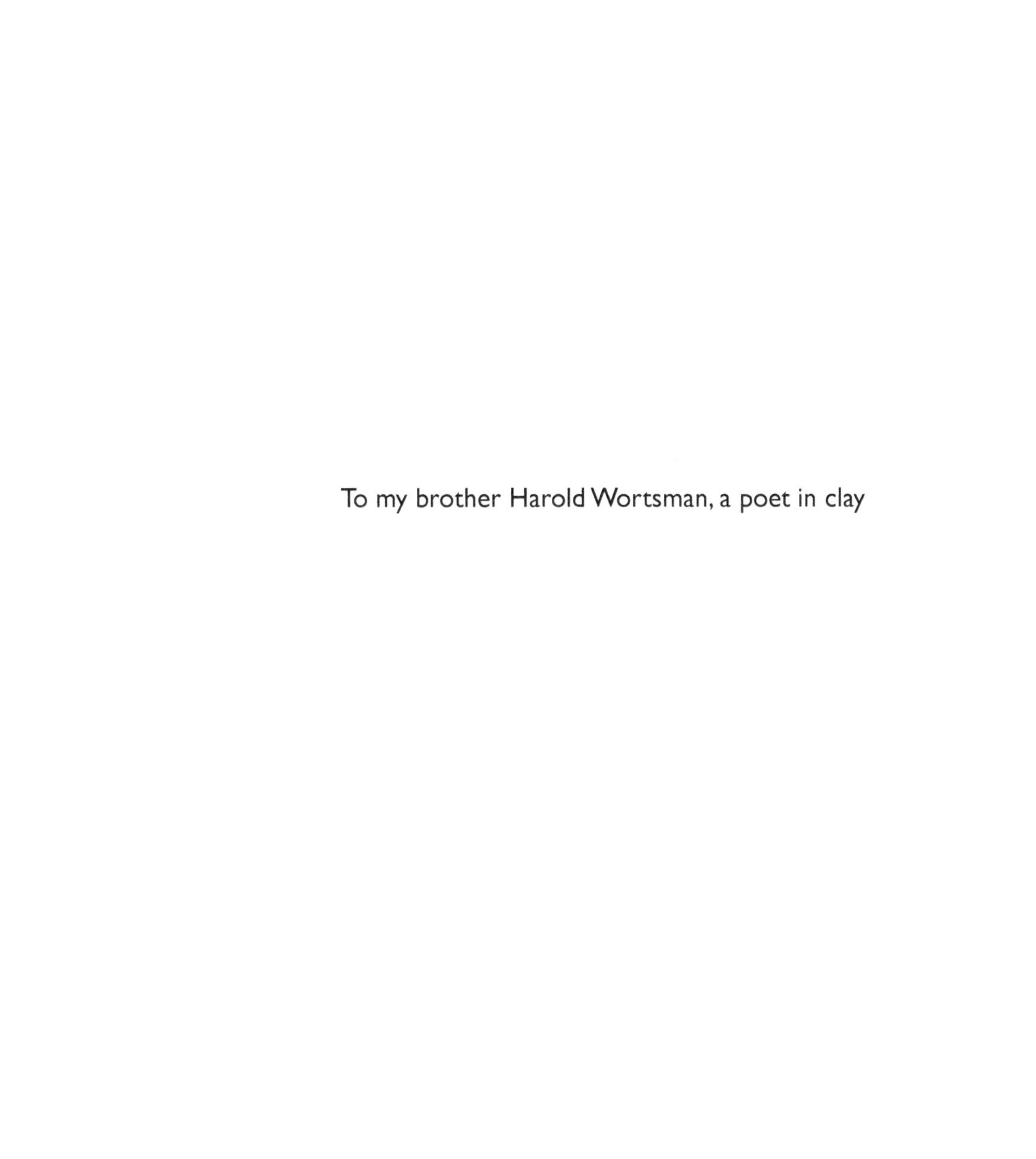

To my brother Harold Wortsman, a poet in clay

Contents

Instructions to Reader

(a found foreword)[1]

1 This text was found in the trash in the Reading Room at the New York Public Library, and a bit tinkered with.

INSTRUCTIONS TO READER
(a slightly modified, found foreword)

Read

carefully!

Bear down firmly when writing

and provide all!

Do not detach!

Return it with the book!

Thereafter

remain visible

until the book is discharged!

And adhere to

no

classics!

Take the A Train!
(A Preface)

The cover image of this book of cut-up poems and collages is a photograph of a piece of found torn art,[2] perfectly composed, set slightly off-center, in the frame set in a black box attached to the wall, formerly utilized to post official MTA instructions and regulations, that caught my eye at the 168th Street station on the A/C-Train lines. Absent title, signature, or any other form of identification, we must assume that it is either a consequence of natural erosion, the felicitous residue of years of placards pasted one over the other, and then scratched away, to be replaced by yet another, or else pruned, torn and shaped by the discriminating fingers of an individual, or a group of individuals of keen aesthetic sense, adroit at the art of tearing, who wish to remain anonymous. Grateful to chance or to anonymous artistry, in either case delighted to have stumbled on this chef d'oeuvre, I am grateful to happenstance for providing the face of this book.

*

At 31 miles in length, connecting the beaches of Far Rockaway, in Queens, to the urban grit of 207th Street in the Inwood District of

---

2 An ardent snap-shooter of urban found art, I am ever on the lookout for an evocative tear-job of posters on the New York subway and the Paris metro, the underground rapid transit systems that I know best, though I am quite sure the practice happens elsewhere as well. Some affiches are so skillfully rent as to strongly suggest the likelihood of deliberate intent and talented tearing technique coupled with an aesthetic sense, rather than arbitrary vandalism. Or perhaps the unseen hands belong to a band of tear-freaks whose passion it is to ride the underground rails at odd hours, early in the morning or late at night, so as to locate and tear undetected. As with graffiti crews, the vast majority being sloppy amateurs, only a select few poster rippers merit the title of "tear artists."

Upper Manhattan, the A-train runs along the longest subway line in the city. Like Superman, it leaps in a single bound, transporting passengers from the stuffy haste of 59th Street/Columbus Circle at the northern rim of the Midtown frenzy to 125th Street in the beating heart of Harlem, the magical trajectory immortalized by the jazz standard "Take the A Train," the signature tune of the Duke Ellington orchestra.

I myself was disabused of the commonly held misapprehension that the tune was composed by the Duke himself one day on my way to work. Seated in the first car of an A-Train, peering out the front window, mesmerized, as I was in childhood, by the graffiti-covered twists and turns of the tunnel, illuminated by the train's headlights. Whistling the tune to myself, perhaps a decibel or two too loud, I saw in the reflection that I was not alone.

The man seated directly opposite me smiled back.

"Please excuse me!" I said. "Every time I take the A-Train, I can't help but hum that Ellington tune."

The man's smile sagged into a smirk. "The Ellington orchestra played it, but Billy Strayhorn composed it!" he set me straight. "'N I damn sure ought to know, 'cause he was my uncle!"

*

If, as this book's first poem maintains, "we know each other from what we leave behind," I will hope these cut-up words and images bestir a smile or two on the face of the reader and perhaps a knowing nod.

Peter Wortsman

July 11, 2025

I

Fragments of Cryptic Text

looking at what people leave
outside on the street

we know each other from
what we leave behind.

the cut-up shards of

memory,

the wrinkled
written
into
when

tory.   the click-clack of his-

ricocheting through

the "tinny smack" of

time

thought threaded

throughout

treasure

                              indistinguishable from
the trash.

Looking at What People Leave
Outside on the Street

        We know each other from

what we leave behind:

        the cut-up shards of

memory,

        the wrinkled

        written

        into

        when,

the click-clack of history

        ricocheting through

the "tinny smack" of

        time,

thought threaded

throughout,

        treasure

indistinguishable from

        the trash.

Poem

poems
    start somewhere;

      thought
       bits

    fertile

     relics

obsessions,

    flaws

      of
      felt
      life,

    inner
      need

things

    simply
      said,

    chaos
     edited
to the bone.

    the anarchy of language
      running
  a joy ride
    an orgy of
uninhibited scattering
      calls

  the voice of God,

A poem is

    pitiless text,

  when it ends,

    resembling
     silence.

Poem

Poems
>start somewhere:

>>>thought
>>>>bits,

>fertile
>>relics,

obsessions,
>flaws
>>of
>>felt
>>life,

>inner
>>need,

things
>simply
>>said,

>chaos
>>edited
>>to the bone,

the anarchy of language
running
a joy ride,
an orgy of
uninhibited scattering
calls,

the voice of God.
A poem is
pitiless text,

when it ends
resembling
silence.

Chaos: Making

laughter, rolling

everywhere —

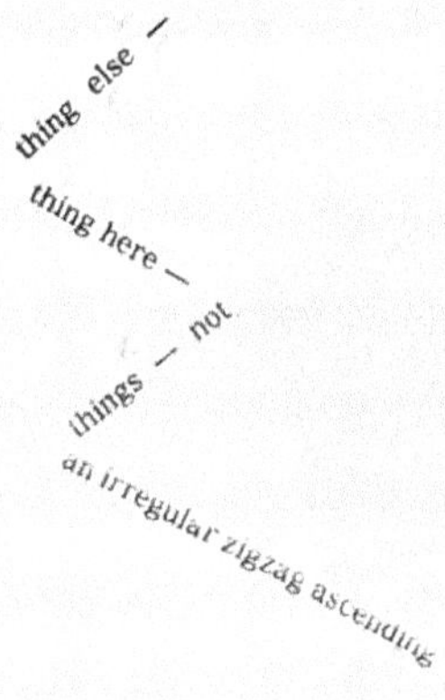

bit of paper
text,

tributary of the Styx,

Paradox: External

Navigating the Not

Chaos making.

laughter rolling

everywhere --

                                                 e
                                               s
                                            l
                                          e
                                           g
                                        n
                                      i
                                    h
                                  t
                                 •
                                  t
                                    h
                                      i
                                        n
                                          g

                                            h
                                              e
                                               r
                                                 e
                                                    °
                                                     t
                                                    o
                                                 n
                                               s
                                             g
                                           n
                                         i
                                       h
                                     t
                                   ■
                                     a
                                       n

                    i
                     r
                      r
                       e
                        g
                         u
                          l
                           a
                            r
                              z
                               i
                                g
                                 z
                                  a
                                   g
                                    g
                                   n
                                  i
                                 d
                                n
                               e
                              c
                             s
                            a

bits
of
text,

          tributary
          of
          the
          River Styx,
          paradox eternal.

lurid   meditation .

We humans
are scientists and storytellers,

consciousness,
the machines

an absurd animal,

a screaming baboon —

with

long-held delusions

of

wisdom.

If nothing else,

a dazzling assortment of
wild propositions

thoughts loose and open-ended.

, but

Why belabor such flaws?

clueless. Blissful,

totally manic and absurd

. Human curiosity is a powerful force,

Lurid Meditation

We humans
are scientists and storytellers,
consciousness machines,
absurd animals
a screaming baboon –
with
long-held delusions
of
wisdom,
if nothing else,
a dazzling assortment of
wild propositions,
thoughts loose and open-ended.
But
why belabor such flaws?

Clueless, blissful,
totally manic and absurd,

human curiosity is a powerful force.

pursuit of
fearsome
paradigm

I don't presume

to know

the Breath of God

to eavesdrop on

infinity,

spellbound by

the Voice

of

THE ANGEL OF DEATH

raw
red
loud

playing at peak intensity,

a

banner finale

on

the instrument
time

but

I'm in no rush,

Not

to

be

Pursuit of a Fearsome Paradigm

I don't presume

to know

the breath of God,

to eavesdrop on

infinity;

spellbound by

the voice

of

the angel of death,

raw,

red,

loud,

playing at peak intensity,

a

banner finale

on

the instrument time,

but

I'm in no rush,

not

to

be

Principles of the Internal[3]

There is no
given.

Suffering needs
knowledge-
tinged
taste and dread.

Fears borne
possess shape.

It is not enough to
lie well,
the trap is laid.

Utter doubt,
avoid
ideas
as needed.

History seeks,
as if it were foreseen,

---

3 Vertical reading from *Harrison's Principles of Internal Medicine*, 21st Edition, by Loscalzo, Fauci, Kasoer and Hauser, McGraw Hill / Medical, 2022

the specter of the
trite,
this
expiatory
recital.

Immune to dark forebodings,
bacteria have a destiny too.

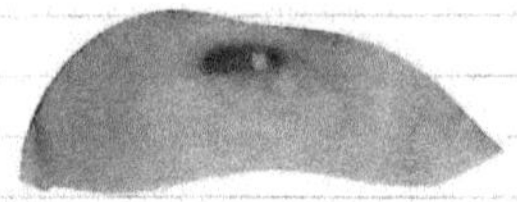

noticing things,

scribe,
with adrenaline,

with

ears, distracted innocent

my eye, and I

collect

all

manner of
mantras.

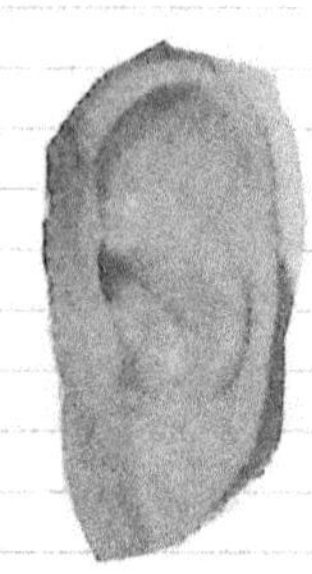

dreams
talking

otherworldly
words, the flowers grow
roots

spirits and miracles

iridescent,
sparkles of

Unexpected epiphanies.

the rust of

wisdom,

bald ing!
with
Buddha belly.

I'm also a real person.

"Sometimes I lie awake and
just listen," i

i don't get bored

Noticing Things

Scribe

with adrenalin

with

ears, distracted innocent.

My eye and I

collect

all manner of mantras:

dreams talking

otherworldly

words, the flowers grow roots,

spirits and miracles,

iridescent sparkles of unexpected epiphanies,

the rust of

wisdom.

Balding

with

Buddha belly,

I'm also a real person.

Sometimes, I lie awake and

I don't get bored.

fragments of cryptic text,

those cruel words

Take a smidgen of

nothingness,
an intangible

pilgrimage

meandering
's eyes,

shock of
sweltering
recoil

there is no singing in hell,

Fragments of Cryptic Text

Those cruel words --

Take a smidgen of

nothingness,

an intangible

pilgrimage,

meandering

eyes,

shock of

sweltering

recoil.

There is no singing in hell.

II

Amid the Din: Visual Poetry and Verbal Collages

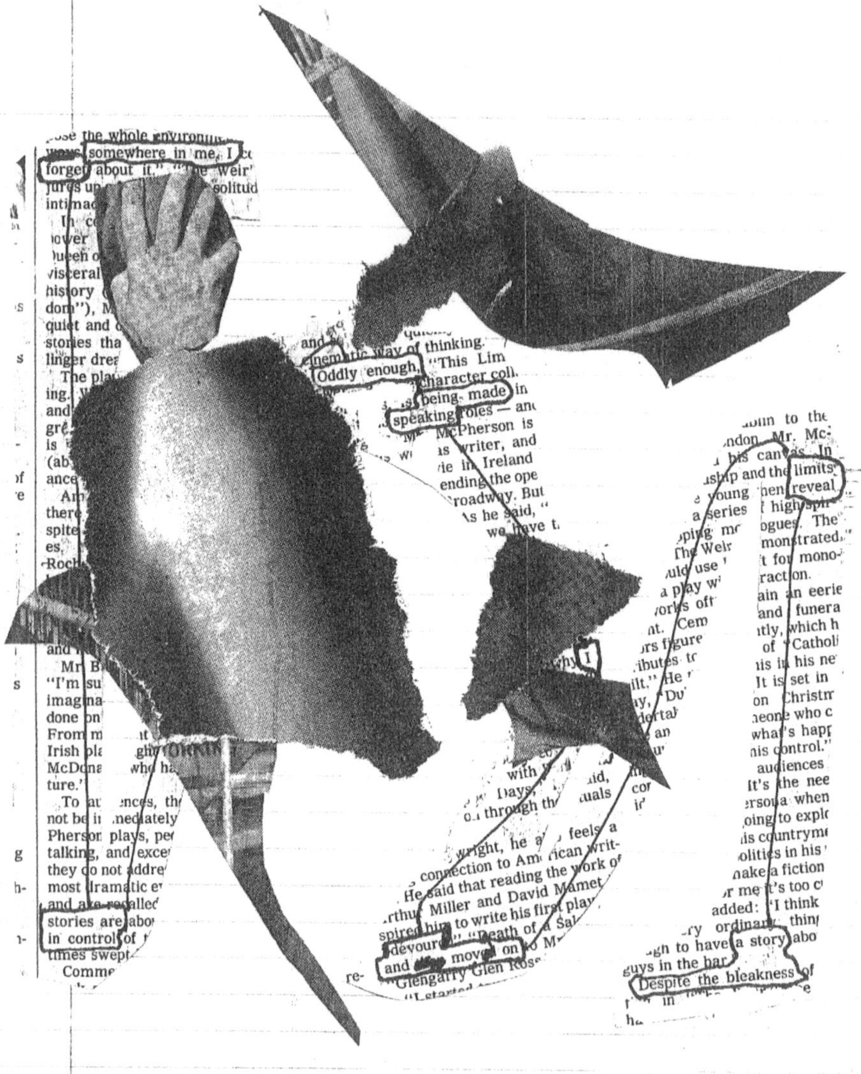

APRIL 1, 1999

Limits Reveal

Somewhere in me, I
forget:

stories are
In control.

Oddly enough,
being made
speaking,
I
devour
and move on.

Limits
reveal

a story,
despite the bleakness.

April 1, 2019

where she is
direction may
"Fable" and
our Alarm F

The curving road fr
the Basilica of St. F
pilgrim's path for r
the air is pasture sweet; in w
stinging. Francis himself, native son an
inclined to joyousness took pleasure in bot
sons.

et on its aqueductlike arches,
is death in 1226 and houses
t flower of a radical n
es by Giotto

church
But with much
ring from the disaster,
or rebuilding is spread th
ntion to the the situati
as to showcase a remark
was temporarily out
tan Museu

don houses.
And they are
gifts to the basili
Europe to honor a
ing, who wan
who live
rty.
is born
hant fa
n ev for
ch at the ti
and erotic, of
le soon uror

Fable

The curving road

the stinging

inclined to joyousness

pleasure in

flower.

Honor

the

erotic

now.

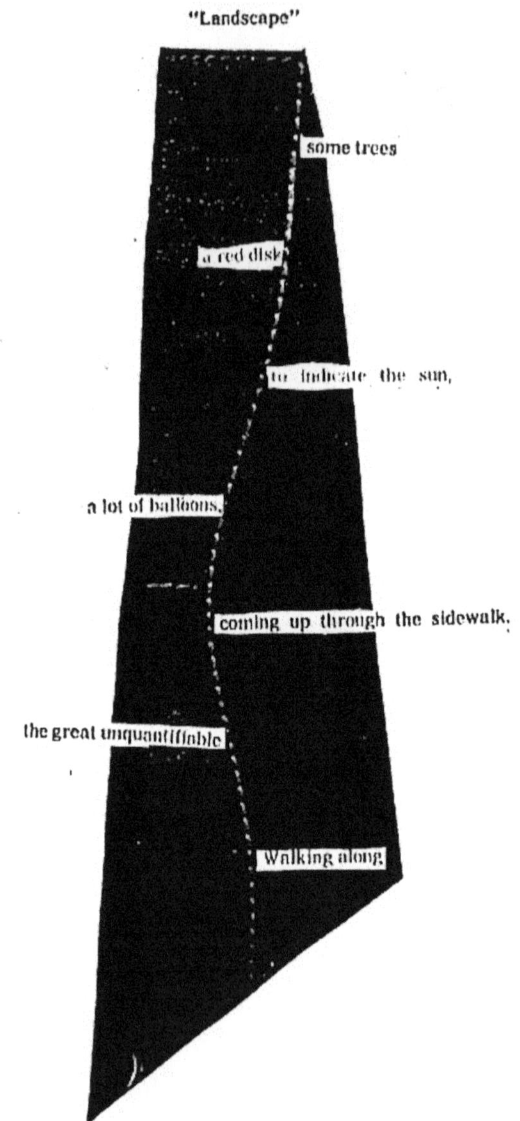

"Landscape"
some trees
a red disk
to indicate the sun,
a lot of balloons,
coming up through the sidewalk,
the great unquantifiable
Walking along

Landscape

some trees

a red disk

to indicate the sun

a lot of balloons

coming up through the sidewalk

the great unquantifiable

walking along

influential
fragilities.

an   experiment in form.

this poem is not,
living .
thought,
turned into
things   an ode to
— The
never forgotten
long ago   ripe
wit,

like a dog   play.   part
but   "I
play.

Reading   it knows

the   Everything is ,

raw
not

mirror
beautiful,
unknowing,
bouncing
to the next

APRIL 20, 2025

40

Influential Fragilities
(an experiment in form)[4]

<pre>
                    This poem is not
         living   an ode to
       thought
       turned into   ripe
                                                    wit;

        things.
--The
never forgotten   part
long ago,
        I,
like a dog   play   it knows
                                 but
                               play
reading   everything
     the
                                                  is
     raw,   not
          mirror   beautiful,
        unknowing,
                              bouncing
            to the next
</pre>

April 20, 2025

---

4 This poem can be read clockwise or counter-clockwise.

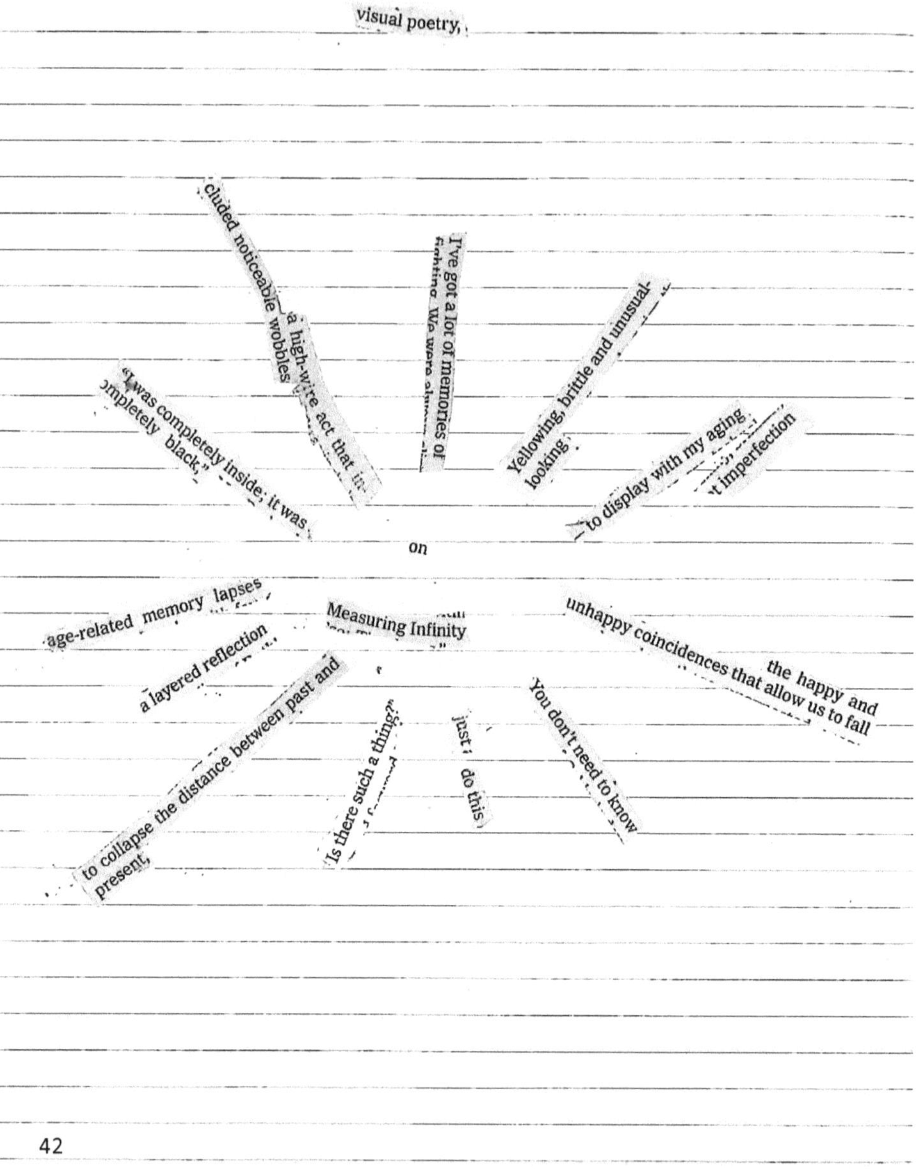
cluded noticeable a high-wire act that in
"I was completely inside; it was
completely black,"
wobbles
I've got a lot of memories of
fighting. We were alw
Yellowing, brittle and unusual-
looking
to display with my aging
t imperfection
on
age-related memory lapses
a layered reflection
Measuring Infinity
unhappy coincidences that allow us to fall
the happy and
to collapse the distance between past and
present,
Is there such a thing?"
just do this
You don't need to know

*Toddler Trapped in a Texas Well
Sings Amid Din of Rescue Effort*

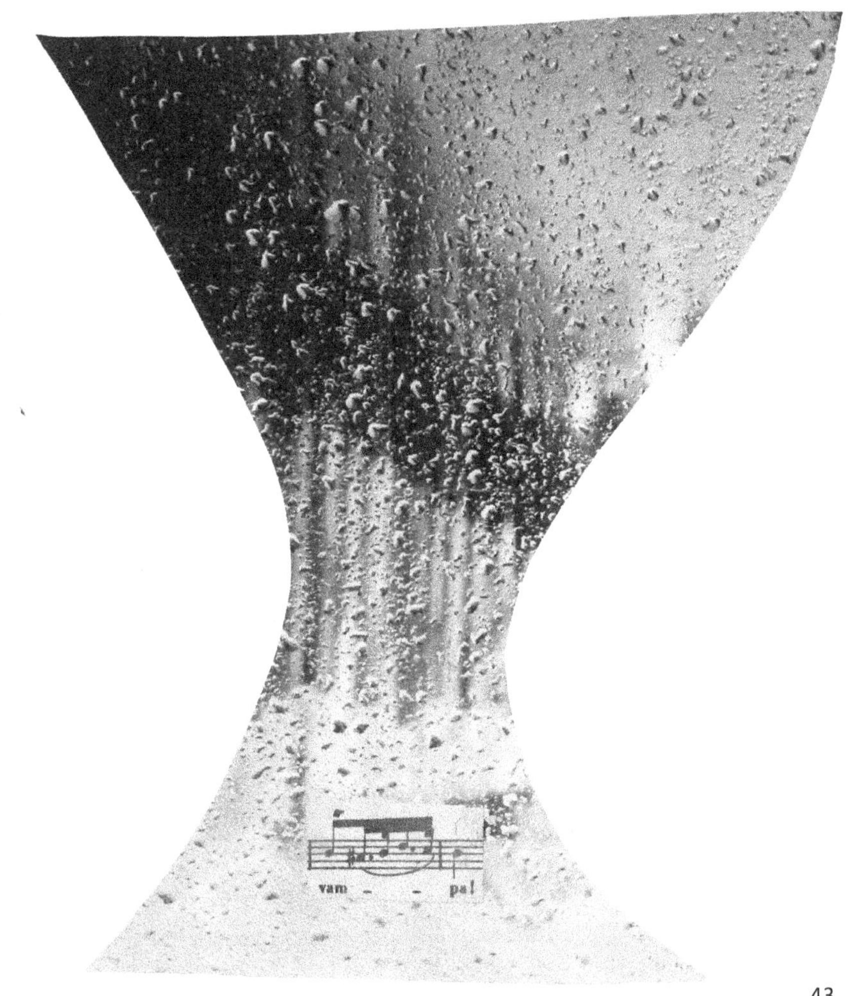

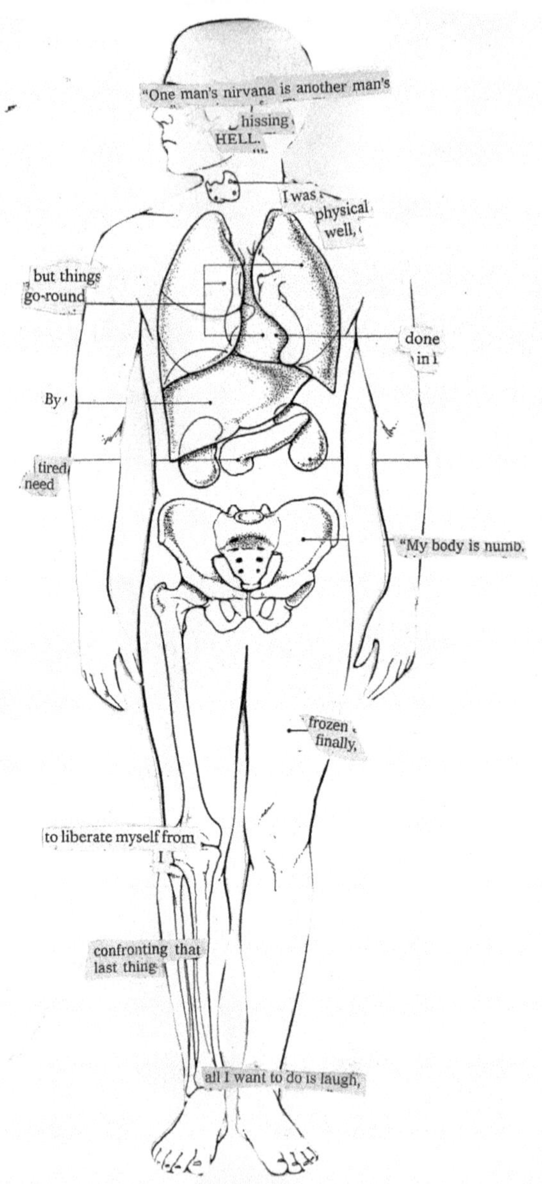

"One man's nirvana is another man's
hissing
HELL.
I was
physical
well,
but things
go-round
done
in l
By
tired
need
"My body is numb.
frozen
finally,
to liberate myself from
I
confronting that
last thing
all I want to do is laugh,

One Man's Nirvana is Another Man's Hissing Hell

                        I was
                                physically
                                        well,
        but things
        go-round;
                                done
                                in

        by

        tired
        need,
                                        my body is numb,

                                frozen
                                finally,

        to liberate myself from
        confronting that
        last thing —

                                all I want to do is laugh.

III

Word Doodles

1.
7, an.
dscape.
)il paint1.
smaller
.ills, and
urch's H
.l elsewl
. life-si7
.itub to
:oncer
attan .
apocaly.
.bove and
ers on the .
f the subway
iistic pranks
)le while the su
ll are treated
high-keyed wa:
tify as the sec(
Expressionis1
e that, it is b
ities of his (
' in cityscaj
paintings
y the w
– woul
'. Wh
rol,
ha

y

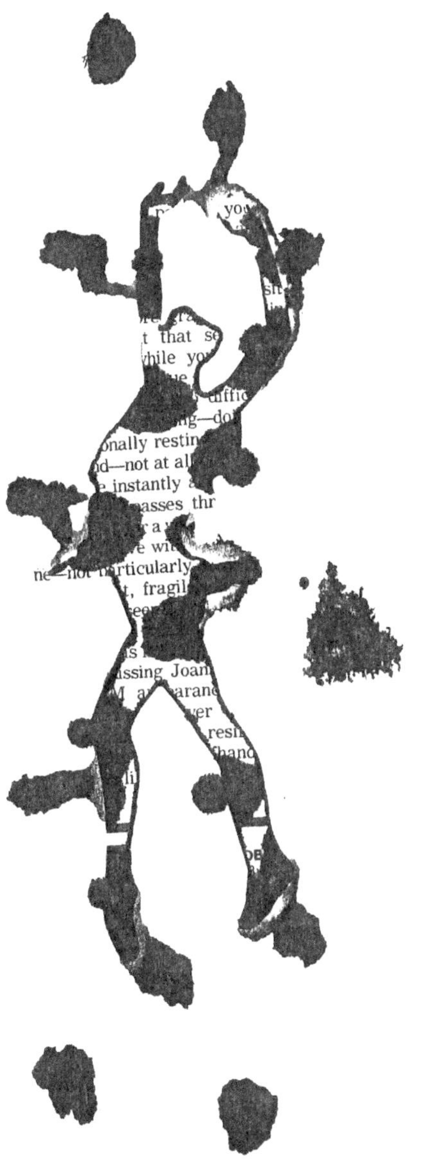

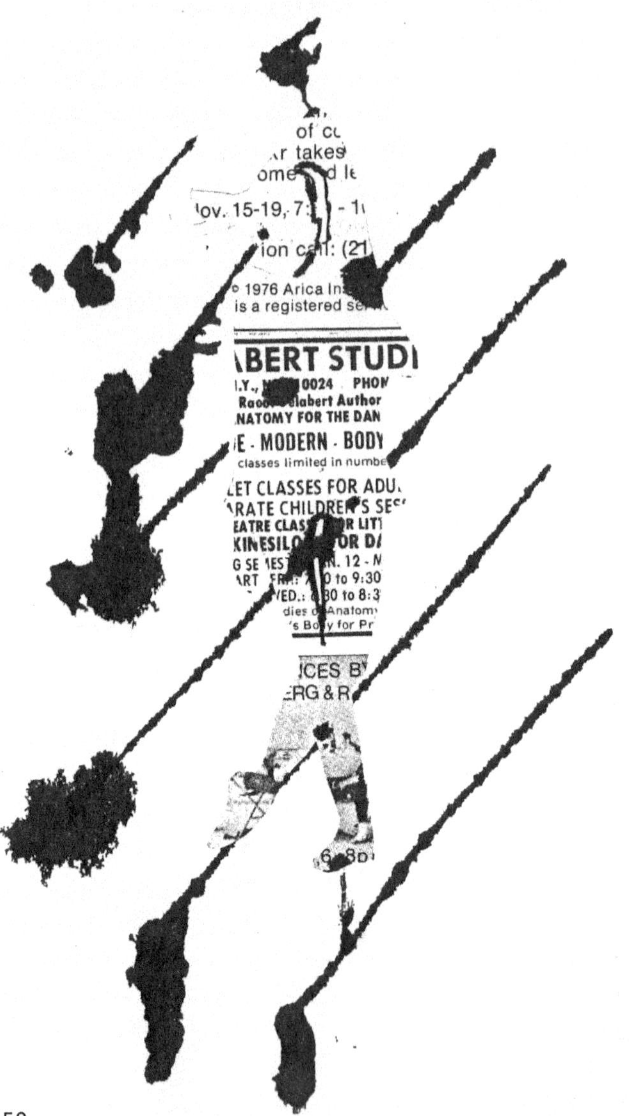
of c
r takes
ome d le
Nov. 15-19, 7: - 1
ion call: (21
© 1976 Arica In
is a registered se
ABERT STUDI
.Y., 0024 PHON
Raoo abert Author
ANATOMY FOR THE DAN
E · MODERN · BODY
classes limited in numbe
ET CLASSES FOR ADU
RATE CHILDREN'S SE
EATRE CLASS OR LITT
KINESILO OR D
G SE 1EST N. 12 - N
ART FR 0 to 9:30
VED.: 30 to 8:3
dies Anatom
s Body for Pr
ICES B
ERG & R
6 8

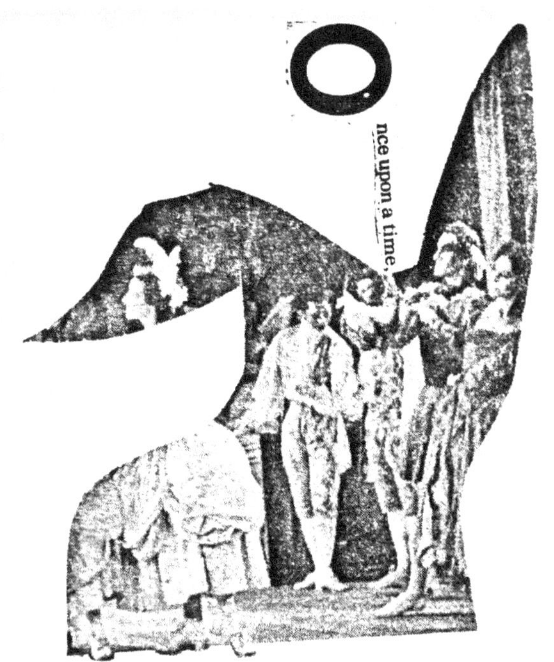

atterns. The
buoyancy: s
ack to e
d fall,
e foot
he spri
f the
ing o
he m
ear
lized
espe
syl
nd
nd
osi

singing with
you feel a pun
hat these ele
ectacles must
ry audiences.
odes, the Fre
ve been quit
company wil
te on Septer

ork Dan
the Bessi
he first
oistero
babies
ed,
d

IV

18 Recycled Epigrams

18 recycled epigrams

1

presented as an oasis surrounded by a
moat of blood,

I was sometimes aware that I wasn't.

2

a hand in writing,

I tear this delicate fabric—Am I

3

There are unsettling ironies here.

If we were to believe .

4

the privacy of suffering

formalistic pleasure in itself .

5

Tension
a delayed land

lingo: segments such as
Listening,"

6

homes
hotels,
crowded trains and perilous
buses,

"When you are in hiding," he said,
"nothing seems safe"

7

eyes. On clear days,

bend rendering.

8

he said. "All it'll do is give you a brain
cramp."

"Oh no," she said, "nothing is more
American."

9

As I travel around, watching

amounts of air.

10

But this is all wrong,

lacking a clear way of presenting,

11

    **Dream is usually thought
fairy tale,
pretext**

"They just keep their eyes open."

12

    believe,
beyond doubt,

    do anything. The confusion lies in the
fact.

13

with death—
We *do*
when needed,
too quickly

like an afterthought,
far more evocative.

14

almost complete and long-buried

I never planned to be.

15

waiting for chaos.

return to bare rock.

16

pained, per-
plexed and passionate as called for.

You said almost nothing.

brain, I can hardly avoid leaping

I can name today.

18

Readers
down the road

Not everything is sweetness.

18 Recycled Epigrams

1

Presented as an oasis surrounded by a
moat of blood,
I was sometimes aware that I wasn't.

2

A hand in writing,
I tear this delicate fabric – am I?

3

There are unsettling ironies here
if we were to believe.

4

The privacy of suffering,
formalistic pleasure in itself.

5

Tension,
a delayed land,
long segments such as
listening.

6

Homes,

hotels,

crowded trains and perilous

busses.

"When you are in hiding," he said,

"nothing seems safe."

7

Eyes on clear days

bend rendering.

8

He said: "All it'll do is give you a brain

cramp."

"Oh, no," she said, "nothing is more

American."

9

As I travel around, watching

amounts of air.

10

But this is all wrong,

Lacking a clear way of presenting.

11

Dream is usually thought,

fairy tale,

pretext.

"They just keep their eyes open."

12

Believe

beyond doubt!

Do anything. The confusion lies in the

fact.

13

With death –

we do

when needed

too quickly,

like an afterthought,

[but] far more evocative.

14

Almost complete and long-buried,

I never planned to be.

15

Waiting for chaos,
return to bare rock.

16

Pained, per-
plexed and passionate, as called for,
you said almost nothing.

17

Brain, I can hardly avoid leaping,
I can name today.

18

Readers
down the road,
not everything is sweetness.

An Inkling of Eternity in my Father-in-Law's Garden
(An Afterword)
(*Pour Auguste*)

Sleep takes hold among the butterflies slipping silently between the leaves, beneath the tall trees in my father-in-law's garden, where he mounted a bed of moss on a big flat rock laid lengthwise, beside which, according to his wishes, his ashes were strewn.

A clap of thunder from somewhere faraway wrests me back into the moment, bathed in sweat and a surge of memory. From that same perch I witnessed long ago my wife's uncle enthroned on a tractor, leading home a herd of sheep on the road that passes behind the school; and after him, his son going the same way, the two long-since deceased. The father distilled a divine pear brandy of which I sipped the last drops. The son made me the precious gift of a black truffle he himself had dug up, and of a woodcock, rare bird nowadays.

I want to grow old here and one day fall asleep for good, lingering maybe for a moment in someone's memory, before, like a fallen leaf, feeding the mulch of tomorrow.

About the Author

Author of work in multiple modes, including fiction, plays, poetry, and translation from the German, most recently *Odd Birds & Fat Cats, An Urban Bestiary*, created in collaboration with his daughter, artist-illustrator Aurélie Bernard Wortsman, short listed for an Eric Hoffer Book Award, Peter Wortsman was a fellow of the Fulbright (1973) and Thomas J. Watson Foundations (1974), and a Holtzbrinck Fellow at the American Academy in Berlin (2010). His work has garnered a Beard's Fund Short Story Award (1985) and an Independent Publishers Book Award (2014), among other honors.

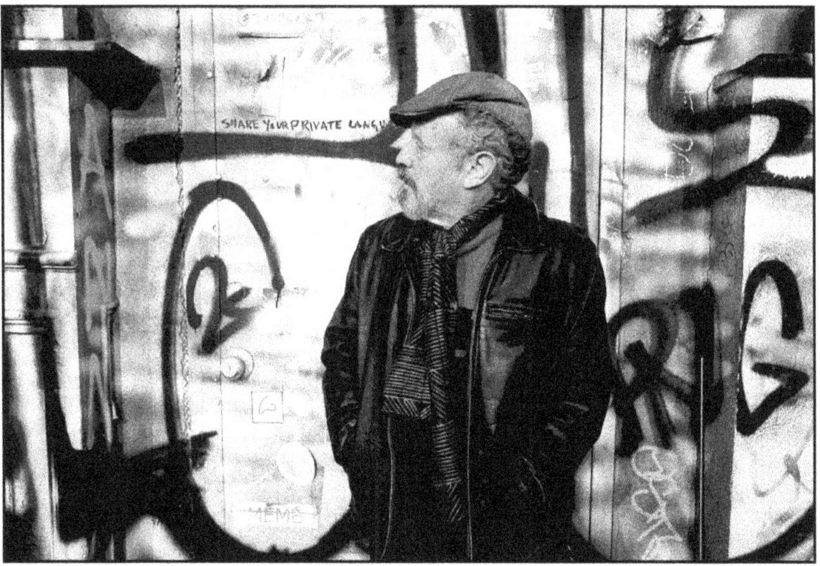

PHOTOGRAPH BY JEAN-LUC FIEVET

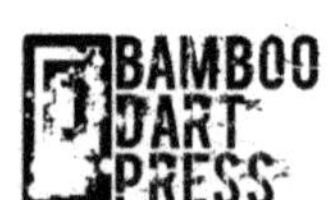

112 N. Harvard Ave. #65

Claremont, CA 91711

chapbooks@bamboodartpress.com

www.bamboodartpress.com